A selection of rhymes based on the
experiences of a long life

❧

SELECTED Poems

Ernst-Wilhelm Friedrich Peters

A selection of rhymes based on the
experiences of a long life

❧

SELECTED Poems

MEMOIRS
Cirencester

Published by Memoirs

MEMOIRS
PUBLISHING

1A The Wool Market, Dyer Street, Cirencester, Gloucestershire, GL7 2PR
info@memoirsbooks.co.uk www.memoirspublishing.com

Selected Poems

ISBN: 978-1-86151-079-2

To my wife

PREFACE

If you were to ask me:" Are you a poet?" My answer in all probability would be "No". I have never followed the rules of poetry, but write verse as it comes into my mind. If you were to ask me, "Do you write rhymes?" I would say "Yes". The following verses are a selection of my poems. They come mostly from experiences of my long life.

I started writing this type of verse when I was a child at school in Germany, and I was always encouraged by my parents and teachers to do so. Much of what I wrote then has been lost, but some of it remained in my mind. I was always encouraged to read the work of our great German poets, and those of other nationalities, hence my love for poetry.

I hope that you will enjoy these few selected poems.

Oh muses of the ancient arts
Inspire me to pen a book of rhyme
That will be enjoyed by many to come
And survive the sands of time.

CONTENTS

THE ENGLISH LANGUAGE

When I arrived in this country
I was always very cautious
When people tried to talk to me
As my English was atrocious.

My grammar wasn't bad at all,
But like most people of my nation
I lacked in vocabulary,
And had awful pronunciation.

A window was always a vindow,
A vest was always a west,
A jam jar was always a yam yar,
A jest always sounded like yest.

That is many years ago now,
I must have improved a lot,
As people very often ask:
"Are you Irish, or are you a Scot?"

My English has much improved by now
Especially my pronunciation,
But the most important fact for me
Is to be part of this ancient nation.

TO MY DARLING

The roaring sound of the deep blue sea
To me is like a symphony
That goes on throughout eternity
And sings of my love for thee.

The roaring sound of the autumn wind
Is the greatest orchestration
It stirs the thoughts within my mind,
And fires the imagination.

I imagine being by the sea
With the autumn wind in my hair
I imagine you to be with me
And love being everywhere.

A QUESTION

You ask me why I love you
I ask "Why do you love me?"
The answer to your question is here,
As you no doubt will see.

I loved you from the early days
Of many years ago,
Your sparkling brown eyes and lovely smile
Did set my heart aglow.

You kept fanning these early flames
When you became my wife,
Making me love you more and more
Throughout our married life.

We are much older now, you and I,
But the embers are still alive
Are still being fanned, my darling,
My dearest loving wife.

How can you ask me why I love you
When you have known like me
That I shall always love you
As much as you love me?

OUR ANNIVERSARY

Life is not always full of fun,
It's like the mighty sea,
It lifts you up to the top of the wave,
And it drops you as fast as can be.

Our life together has been like that,
Many times we were dropped down,
But we had many times on the crest of the wave
As we moved from town to town.

However there was always something
That was there for you and me,
'twas our constant love for each other
From the start to eternity.

Today is once again special,
It's our anniversary,
Let's hope there are many more of these
For both of us, you and me.

CHRISTMAS EVE 2010

Do you remember Christmas Eve of 1948?
I got up early so not to be late
For this most important day of my life,
When we stood at the altar of a small village church
To be joined as husband and wife.

Many Christmas Eves have passed since then,
Today makes it sixty-two,
And all those years of our lives
You loved me as I loved you.

We have grown old together now,
Husband and wife,
And we can look back on all those years
Of happy married life.

Today on our anniversary,
Like all those that have gone before
I just want to say: "Thank you darling,
I shall love you for evermore".

ON OUR SIXTY-THIRD WEDDING ANNIVERSARY

December has come once again,
There are no more leaves on the trees,
No more chirping of friendly songbirds,
No more humming of wasps and bees.

Christmas Eve is not far away
An important day of our life,
For sixty-three years ago on this day
You became my loving wife.

As Christmas presents come and go
This was the most precious one
That we gave to each other years ago
My only lovely one.

We never tired of this present
It never wore out or got lost,
We unwrapped it anew, year after year
At very little cost.

Now today I say it once again
Like it shall always be,
Our love for one another:
Happy Anniversary.

HAPPY ANNIVERSARY

You are laughter, you are fun.
You are the moon, you are the sun
You are the anchor in the sea of life
You are my darling, my sweetheart,
My lover, you're my wife.

It is sixty-four years to the day
Since you and I were wed.
It is sixty-four years to the day
That you became my Ed.

It is sixty-four years to the day
That our journey began,
And you my darling Eddy
Made me a happy man.

What else can I say, my darling?
Thank you for all those happy years,
I am hoping that there will be many more
Without worries and without fears.

OLD LOVE

Now I am old there is many a night
When I can't sleep very well.
My mind keeps wandering round and round
Insomnia can be hell.

I think of all the sights I have seen,
All the people I have met,
Of all the places to which I have been,
Of what I might see yet.

My mind goes back to when we first met,
To those days of long ago
When walking with you holding hands,
Our young hearts with love aglow.

Here we are lying next to each other
Even in sleep holding hands,
You are breathing gently, I can't sleep,
Waiting for night to end.

We've travelled together for many a year,
But often I feel so afraid
I feel you are leaving me bit by bit,
As I see your memories fade.

It bothers me that the day might come
When you won't know me any more,
But please don't fear, I'll always be here,
As I have promised before.

I think and think, sleep will not come,
Its getting light outside,
The dawn chorus will be starting soon,
Then I notice your eyes open wide.

"How did you sleep?" you ask me,
I answer "Very well",
But you won't know I'm lying,
Because you slept so well.

Finally it is daytime,
The long night is o'er
I shall always try to look after you
The same as I did before.

I hope and pray that I shall always be fit
To care for you all your life,
I love you so much, and I know you love me,
My dearest loving wife.

YOUNG LOVE

The fog was settling that night,
I was walking like in a dream,
The narrow streets and lanes
Led me to the old familiar stream,
The gaslights lighting up the scene
Shed circles of golden light
It was one of those peaceful places
To be at that very night

I was on my way to meet you,
My very first real date,
I knew I was much too early,
But better early then late.
We had met a couple of days before,
Two youngsters still at school,
But we thought we were in love.
I know I was just a fool.

We met up at the bulwark
By the side of the old stream,
We seemed to walk miles on that foggy night
Holding hands was love's young dream.
We heard the foghorns of the ships
That into the harbour came,
It was a night to remember
Life would never be the same.

At least that was what we thought,
My lovely young lady and I,
When we parted that evening
We felt like wanting to cry.
We gave each other a little hug
When we said good night at her door,
I also stole a little kiss,
I had never done that before.

I went on my way, I didn't walk
I floated like on a cloud,
I thought of the lovely night we had,
And kept on singing aloud.
I am a lucky fellow
And I think I am in love,
My thanks to you, whosoever you are
Somewhere up above.

After that we met a few more times
It was not like the first blissful night,
The romantic scene of the dark foggy day
Was forgotten when we had a fight.
She met other boys, I met other girls,
We both went our own way,
But the memory of that romantic date in the fog
Will never go away.

I never knew what happened to her,
Does she remember that night
Now more then seven decades ago,
When we were young and bright?

DEAR JOHN,
A CHRISTMAS TALE

One Christmas he received her letter.
She simply wrote: "Dear John,
I wish you a happy Christmas,
It is two years since you have gone.

I don't know when you will come back,
Or if I shall see you again,
We had some good times in the past,
But in the past they shall remain.

I cannot wait any longer
I met another guy,
Merry Christmas and a Happy New Year,
Goodbye.

He read her words over and over,
Tears standing in his eyes,
He had loved her all this time
Now there were just goodbyes.

Another part of life was over,
It would never, never return,
He read each of her letters
Before in the stove they would burn.

In the long run it all turned out well
For John had a change of life,
When he was released from the prison camp
He met his most wonderful wife.

OLD AGE

I am a feline geriatric,
My coat is all shiny and black,
Sitting here in the window
I can't help looking back
To the days when I was a kitten,
When the world was all full of fun,
When my mother and I, in the days now gone by
Chased rabbits and mice on the run.

My father they say was ugly,
A monster all shiny and black,
Always feeding and fighting for what it was worth
With a big jagged scar on his back.
It was said that he got it one autumn
When he was out chasing a toad,
He forgot to look left, and forgot to look right
As he chased it right over the road.

He woke up at the veterinary surgeon's
Who lived quite near in the town,
He snarled at the man bending over him
In his cap and his mask and his gown.
"What's the matter with me?" growled my father,
"I'm feeling all stiff and I'm sick!"

"That's right", said the veterinary,
"You'd better get better quick,
For once let this please be a warning,
Next time you chase after a toad,

Look left and look right, and prick up your ears
Before you cross over the road".

So the old man got himself better,
But life was never the same,
No more feeding and fighting and growling at vets
No more chasing or playing a game.

Now I sit here like the old man,
With my coat still shiny and black,
But like all feline geriatrics
All I can do is look back.

TOBY'S DILEMMA

I woke up this morning having had a good night,
When I opened my eyes I had such a fright,
No one had drawn the curtains,
Someone had switched off the lights.

I heard a voice saying: "Come in and see,
I don't think my eyes are deceiving me
Something is wrong with our cat
We must take him to the vet".

They took me to see the local vet,
Who said: "Now let me see,
I shall take a sample of his blood,
And check your Toby's BP".

She took some blood and checked my BP,
A procedure I did not like,
I thought to myself, I wish she would stop,
And get off on her bike.

She looked into my eyes with a bright light
Muttered to herself and said: "Ah,
I know what's wrong with your pussy
He has a detached retina."

I wondered what that was,
Wherever did she find
A word like that,
Why didn't she say "He is blind"?

So my life will undergo changes
I shall bump into walls and doors
And any forgotten obstacles
That are lying on the floor.

Never mind, I'm a strong-willed cat,
And even if I am blind
I shall defy this infirmity
And a way round my home I shall find.

However, I am grateful,
Even if I am just a cat,
Thank you for your kindness
My lovely lady vet.

TOBY THE PATIENT

I have been to the vet again
In a way it's a bit of a pain,
But she said I shall be fine
"Keep taking the Amlodipine".

My blood pressure is much lower,
My kidneys are much better,
The renal diet is doing the trick
As long as I don't get fatter.

I am so glad he fetched me home,
I had enough being cooped up,
I really missed my freedom,
And I certainly missed my grub.

Here I am at home at last,
I don't like visiting the vet,
"See you in three months' time"
She said. "You want a bet?"

They say it is a dog's life,
But what do they really know?
They should try being a cat for once,
That is always on the go.

Perhaps then they will understand
What it is like to be locked up
Without a garden to roam about
And forbidden to have some grub.

I am old now and I have lost my sight,
But when I am out here I feel free,
I still put rabbits and rats to flight
Even if I cannot see.

Now here is my message to all felines,
Never give up the good fight,
You can still enjoy a very good life
Even if you lose your sight.

FAREWELL TO TOBY

The twenty-second of January
Was a very sad day
It was the last day of your life,
The day you went away.

You have been with us for a long time,
In fact for fifteen years
And you have always had our love,
Through happy days and fears.

The first time that we saw you
In our daughter's house
You were so tiny and noisy,
Just like a little mouse.

We loved you as soon as we saw you,
And we took you away to our home,
Which is in the middle of the countryside
With plenty of space to roam.

You loved to run about
And cross the road to the farm
And every time you crossed it
You never came to harm.

You used to catch mice and rabbits,
And the occasional fly,
And when you took it into your head
You took a day off far away.

We used to call them awaydays,
Just like people do on the train,
But all our calling on those days
Has always been in vain.

You always came back refreshed though,
Not complaining of sunshine or rain,
You often went off for a day or two,
But always came back again.

One year you went away for three weeks,
We called you all the time,
There was no excuse when you came back
Your absence had no reason or rhyme.

Oh Toby, you have been quite unwell,
The last few days have been bad,
We knew that something was wrong with you
We had to call the vet.

She took you away to examine you,
She called me later that day,
She said you had a tumour
She could not take away.

We had a long discussion
To decide what would be for the best,
We listened and took the advice of the vet
To let you have your rest.

You are gone now darling Toby
We are so very sad,
We know that you are grateful
For the life of freedom you had.

Farewell now, our lovely Toby,
Sleep well wherever you be
We know you'll be chasing wildlife
In that great big cattery.

TOBY'S ARRIVAL IN HEAVEN

I have arrived up here now,
The journey took quite a while,
It seemed to go on forever,
Mile after mile.

But now I am here I like it,
It is so cosy and warm,
None of the other pussycats
Are out to do me harm.

They welcomed me and seemed to know
That I had come from Devon.
They said: "Hi Toby,
Welcome to our feline heaven".

There is so much to see and do,
I wonder if I shall have the time
To explore every corner of this place,
But here there is no time,

The food is excellent up here,
I can have chicken every day,
I can have it roasted or chasseur,
At least that's what they say.

I told them that I am used to eating
Any tasty dish,
Except that I am not very fond
Of any kind of fish.

"Don't worry Toby", the head chef said,
"I'll make a note of that,
Because if I don't write it down
It goes right out of my head."

Of course there are some other cats
Who try to mess you about,
I met one only yesterday,
In the distance I heard him shout.

He shouted:" Toby, whatever you want
Be assured I am your man,
I can get you anything,
You bet your life I can."

But I am quite wise to his talk,
I met many like him below,
I simply told him to sling his hook
To bugger off and go.

There are others that are really nice,
Some of them girls, some boys,
They all are really friendly
And tell me of heaven's joys.

I'm sure that I shall like it here,
You know I'm no longer blind,
I have been cured of all ailments
My way around I now find.

So I beg you please don't worry,
I am perfectly all right
I shall look down to earth on you
If I remember every night.

So if you look at the starry sky ,
Remember I'm looking down
Sending cats' meows from my new home
To that lovely Devon town.

Where I once used to roam
Remember all life is without end
It goes on and on through eternity,
In some distant heavenly land.

OUR TOBY

Each morning at the break of day
He stood outside our back door,
Asking for his dish of chicken,
Now he doesn't live here any more.

He left quite unexpectedly
We miss him standing at the door,
All we can say now to ourselves,
"He doesn't live her any more".

His partner little Boko
In the mornings looks at the door,
But all we can ever say to him
"He doesn't live her any more".

Toby's cat friends call for him
Often outside our back door
But all we can ever say to them
"He doesn't live here any more".

Don't ask me where he may be now,
He who stood at our back door,
He has left for a better place
He doesn't live here any more.

He has left his home in Devon,
Has he found another back door
In the place we call cats' heaven
Now he doesn't live her any more?

BOKO'S THOUGHTS

Hi, you have heard of me before,
Toby the big cat was my friend,
We lived together amiably,
Right to the very end.

I still don't understand
Why he suddenly was gone,
But a lady in an ambulance
Took him from our home.

I hope they treat him really well
Where he has been taken to,
Because he does deserve it
I'm sure you think so too.

Well it is over a week now,
Since Toby disappeared,
I don't think he will come back now
It is as I had feared,

I really miss my partner
Who was always ready to fight
And sometimes, I shall admit it
He gave me the odd fright.

Well Toby, my old fellow,
Be lucky wherever you are,
And if you get near the Black Cats' Club
Think of me and have a jar.

I am the number one cat now
In this lovely place in Devon,
And here I shall stay until that day
That we meet again in heaven.

THE TALE OF THE LITTLE BLACK CAT

The people who first gave me a home
Gave me the name Fellini,
I don't know why they called me that
Perhaps 'cos I was teeny.
I didn't live with them very long,
No one ever told me why,
When one day they just took me
To a cattery nearby.

The people there were all very nice,
But it was not a home,
I spent my days in a very small room,
There was little space to roam.
Then one day some people came,
They said "What a pretty black cat,
But hasn't it got a funny name?"
So I thought "Well that is that".

However they said "Just come along,
We shall give you a lovely home".
But there the space was quite confined,
No place for me to roam.
They changed my name to Dempsey,
I thought it a strange name,
I didn't really like it,
It sounded like someone of fame.

But I am just a pussy,
Who longs for a loving home,
Where there is space around me
For me to play and roam.
Alas my luck was out again,
The people said I must go.
"He is too wild and restless
We need a cat that's slow."

So back it was to the cattery
They loved me there I know,
That's where I spent the next nine months,
But time went very slow.

But then one day my luck seemed to change,
A man came to pick a cat.
He was accompanied by a lady,
Who said "Just look at that".
They both looked at me,
I sat up and purred
Hoping they would take me home
From Axhayes Cattery.

I have been here for some time now,
Once again they changed my name.
They simply call me Boko,
But to me its all the same
Fellini, Dempsey or Boko ,
What is there in a name?
As long as I can be happy
Playing and hunting for game.

I have been here for some months now,
With a garden and fields to roam,
At last I have found cat lovers
Who gave me a lovely home.
I love it here and they love me,
And Toby, the other cat
We don't get on too badly
Except for the odd little spat.

I thought I'd like to write this
To let you know about me,
And how I finally settled
As you no doubt can see.
Now for this festive season
Merry Christmas and happy New Year
To all of you at Axhayes
From all of us who live here.

FELINE FANTASIES

"Listen" said Toby to Boko,
"This morning, to my surprise
I heard the man on the radio say
That male mice could harmonise.
Did you know that? I didn't
I know that birds can sing,
But I never heard of singing mice
It must be the latest thing.

Perhaps if some of them got together
And formed a mouse's choir
We could go and see them perform
At the local Cats' Empire.
I suppose we could one Saturday night
If there is nothing else to do,
We could listen to their performance
And perhaps catch one or two.

"I wonder if female mice can sing.
To me it would be no surprise
If I heard it said by someone,
Only male mice can harmonise.
It really would be quite unfair
In this age of equality,
If female mice could sing and dance
Though it would add to the jollity.

Now you are really talking, man,
Just imagine a mouse like Jane Russell,
Or one like Marlene Dietrich,

Or a dancer like Darcy Bussell.
I can see the billboards
Lit up shiny and bright:
"Come to the Cats' Empire
Mouse Choir's Gala Night."

"Just imagine us hearing them singing,
Showing off their attraction,
Jerking about like the Rolling Stones,
Trying to get satisfaction."
"I never liked them very much,
They weren't all that good,
Mick himself was not that bad,
But I couldn't stand Ronnie Wood.

"Imagine them singing in harmony,
Jiggling about their pelvis,
Thinking to themselves all the time
That they are as good as Elvis.
Now if they sing like Rod Stewart,
Or even like Van the Man,
Chris de Burgh or Barry Manilow,
Then I'll definitely go if I can."

FELINE CAPERS

(A Cornish adventure)

Pussy cat, pussy cat, where have you been?
I've been to Cornwall, to Carnhell Green.
Pussy cat, pussy cat, what did you do there?
I had me a pasty, but it tasted quite nasty
So I thought I'd go elsewhere.

I went to a place called Gwinear,
Called in at the pub for some beer,
I didn't wake up until morn,
Then I went to a place called Camborne.

In order to get there I jumped on a bus,
The driver made quite a fuss,
He said to take me there
I'd have to pay a fare.

Once I got to Camborne I thought what a place,
It's not fit for cats, just the human race,
I met a cat that said our lives
Were more suited to a place called St Ives.

So we both went off , this time on a train
Hoping never to see Camborne again.
The train took us to St Erth
There was not much there of any worth.

So we changed again for better lives
Catching a train bound for St Ives.
We were told that on the way to St Ives

We might meet a man who had seven wives,
But we didn't really care,
As long as we got there.

The journey from St Erth to St Ives
Was the loveliest journey of our lives.
The train passed many a sight on the way,
Until we stopped at Carbis Bay.

Now we were almost there,
Some kind cat lover having paid our fare,
Now for a new time of our lives,
Meow! We are at St Ives.

Here we had many a lovely dish
Prepared from tasty, fresh-caught fish
We decided to spend the rest of our lives
In beautiful, cat-friendly, Cornish St Ives.

The moral of the story is,
If you want the time of your lives
Don't go to that place called Carnhell Green
Just go straight on to St Ives.

HEIMWEH

Nun bin ich schon so lange
Von meiner Heimat fort.
Bin hin und her gefahren
Seit Jahren von Ort zu Ort.
Doch durch alle diese Reisen,
Sehr oft bei Tag und Nacht
Hab ich Dich niemals vergessen,
Und immer an Dich gedacht.

Nun wohn ich schon seit Jahren
In einem fremden Land,
Aber oft in meinen Gedanken
Seh ich den Oderstrand.
Ich träume von dem Bollwerk
Und den Brücken, die kreuzen den Fluss,
Und dann sende ich Dir, mein liebes Stettin
Aus der Ferne n'en freundlichen Gruss.

Du hast nun einen anderen Namen
Er ist nicht mehr Stettin,
Was Dein Name war in Deutsch
In Polnisch ist er Szczecin.
Aber was ist schon in einem Namen ?
Die Stadt ist immer noch dort,
Nur die Namen sind jetzt anders
Sonst ist es derselbe Ort.

Für Alle die dort geboren sind
Wird es immer die Heimat sein
Du bist immer in unseren Träumen
Stettin,Szczecin, nur Du allein.

REMINISCENCES

My cradle stood in Pommern
In Eastern Germany,
Where the mighty river Oder
Flows into the Baltic Sea.

My hometown straddles the river
In the East and in the West,
Among the cities of Germany
It was one of the best.

I remember this lovely old city
With its woodlands and meadows of green,
It will always be in my memory
This place known as Stettin.

I remember the river traffic,
With all the ships I have seen
From countries near and far away,
They all came to my Stettin.

I remember the busy bulwark,
The fishwives selling their wares
Which my mother used to buy so often
To provide the most wonderful fare.

I remember the friendly narrow lanes
That to the river led,
The wide streets with their many shops,
The churches with roofs of green lead.

I remember the Sunday mornings
When church bells rang loud and clear,
When people in their Sunday best
Came to church from far and near.

I remember the lovely parks,
Forests in their mantle of green,
The beautiful ancient buildings
That graced my lovely Stettin.

I remember the people we lived with,
People I met at school,
Some sad, others happy, some wise,
Others acting the fool.

I remember the old Duke's Palace,
With its ancient novelty clock,
Theatres, cafés and cinemas,
And ships that lay in the docks.

I remember dear old Sedina
In front of the library,
The old grey garrison church
Next to the cemetery.

There are many things I remember
From the dear old town of my birth
I remember that to me it was
The finest place on earth.

MEMORIES

I walked along the harbour front at Cork
And saw an old familiar scene
That reminded me of a similar place
Where years ago I had been

I looked at the ships at anchor
With their flags orange, white and green,
And then I spotted a coastal tramp
Which had the name 'Stettin'
Written on its stern and prow.
I thought I was in a dream,
But there it was, the ship that like me,
Had come from dear old Stettin.

My thoughts went wild and in my mind
I saw the old Oder stream,
Where I used to walk all those years ago,
It seemed just like a dream.
I saw the parks and the cobbled streets
The people young and old,
I heard their voices and remembered the tales
That once I had been told.

I saw the gaslights on the harbour front,
Heard ships' sirens and stevedores grunt,
I saw lots of sailors coming ashore
And the colourful clothing some of them wore.
All that is many years ago,

Time has flown by like a dream,
I have lived a life on foreign shores,
But still dream of my Stettin.

It is different now,
One no longer hears the same voices in Stettin,
All that was changed many years ago
Now the place is known as Szczecin.

MY POMERANIA

I was born in Pomerania
Where the blue sea laps golden sand
Where dark blue pines watch over the dunes
That sweep down to the strand,
Where the mighty river Oder
Flows into the Baltic Sea,
Where I once lived in a city
That was home sweet home to me.

This city on the Oder
Was once known as Stettin,
But all that changed in forty-five
When its name was changed to Szczecin
The people who lived there at that time
Had to leave their homes behind,
But the thought of home and heritage
Will always be on their mind.

Many years have passed since then,
But we still think of our Stettin,
Where the Oder has flowed through eternity,
Where once our home had been.

DREAMS

I saw the dark blue sea,
The sea and the white sand,
And when I looked round I knew at once
I was back in Pommernland.

I saw pine trees and sand dunes,
I heard familiar sounds
Of gentle breezes and lapping waves,
Peace was all around.

But where were all the people
That once used to live here?
Where had they gone, what made them leave
This land we loved so dear?

Then all at once I saw it,
A seagull, and heard its scream
Which woke me up, and I realised
It had all been just a dream.

MEMORIES OF
WEST CORNWALL

Have you ever been to West Cornwall
On a stormy winter's day?
Have you ever walked on the beach at Hayle
Almost being blown away?
Have you ever felt the wind in your hair?
I did, many years ago,
I was there.

Have you ever been to St Ives Bay
On an early morning in spring?
That was unlike any other day,
Watching curlews on the wing?
Did you see some early daffodils,
And were there dolphins there?
I saw it all many years ago,
I was there.

Have you ever seen the rugged cliffs
On a lovely summer's day?
Have you ever seen bathers on the beach
And sunshine bathing the bay?
Have you ever seen Godrevy
Standing proudly in the sea?
I saw it all many years ago,
It's a wonderful place to be.

SUMMER FAIR AT HAYLE

Lights are flashing, music playing,
People dashing, children saying
One more ride before we go,
Just one more, we love it so.

Daylight is fading, lights still flashing,
Music playing, people dashing
One more ice-cream before we go,
Just one more, we love it so.

It's quite dark now, lights still flashing,
Music playing, people dashing,
Children saying "Let's not go
Not for a while, we love it so!"

Lights are gone now, no more flashing,
All is quiet now, no one dashing,
Children sleeping, breathing slow,
All exhausted, they loved it so.

Fair has gone now, no more flashing,
The site is empty, no people dashing,
Children asking "Why did they go?
Why didn't they stay?
We loved it so."

NORTH CLIFFS AT HAYLE IN THE SUMMER

The sun was shining, the sea was blue
Up on the North Cliffs, just me and you,
Winds blowing softly from the north west
'twas the sort of day that we liked best.

We stood and stared and walked for miles,
Met people with dogs and returned their smiles.
Sails on the horizon out in the west,
'twas the sort of day that we liked best.

Along the footpath we walked and walked,
Admired the scene and the birds and talked,
Stopped and stared at Godrevy, took a rest,
'twas the sort of day that we liked best.

Later on we turned back; it was time to go home,
Seabirds flying about, thoughts ready to roam
To other shores in the west,
'twas the sort of day that we liked best.

EAST DEVON

Let me take you by the hand
And lead you through my promised land
Of winding lanes and rolling hills,
Of ancient trees and daffodils,
Of meadows green that sweep down to the sea,
And let me tell you what it means to me.

I've travelled wide, I've travelled far,
Many places I have seen,
From rocky cliffs to city streets,
To places rough and mean
But at last I know that I have found
The place where I want to be:
My Devon by the sea.

DEVON

I am sure that time has stood still
Since the creation of this land.
There are waters still and deep,
And beaches of golden sand.

There are cattle, horses, wildlife and sheep,
There are people who plough and sow and reap
The deep red soil of this land,
There are people who will always lend a hand
To make this land a heaven,
For all of us who love Devon.

ST ANDREW'S CHURCH, FENITON

The heart of St Andrew's has been beating strong
For about a thousand years,
And it will continue to beat as long
As people worship here.

Who were the people who built the church?
So many years ago?
What was their reason to build it here?
Who can say, we'll never know.

What brought them down to Devon?
Who gave them the motivation?
To settle here in Feniton
To worship the Lord of creation?

St Andrews has weathered many storms,
Storms of nature and storms of man,
And each time the storms had passed
Our church always rose again.

Its heart never stopped its constant beat,
As people always pray
That this church would last for evermore
And their faith would never sway.

Recently St Andrews was damaged by floods
Caused by torrential rain
But the prayers and the will of the people

Made sure it would rise again.
Today as in centuries gone by
We have gathered in celebration
To once again hear the heartbeat
In this act of rededication.

We hope and pray that this ancient church
Will survive for many more years,
As a place of worship for all of us
Without all our worries and fears.

THE HEDGES' TALE

We are two country hedges,
Flanking a Devon lane,
Where we have stood for many years,
Come sunshine or come rain.

Each year we saw the seasons,
Spring, winter, summer and fall,
We saw different generations
Oh yes, we saw them all.

We saw people in the spring of life,
Some of them growing old,
We saw many young and happy,
Others quite distant and cold.

We saw some leaving the village,
For reasons we never knew,
Some of them returned, some never did,
These were luckily very few.

Each year farmers sharpened their hooks
To give us our annual trim
To keep us looking neat and green
And full of vigour and vim

Alas those days are gone now,
No more farmers with sharpened hooks,
They have machines now to trim us,
But they really spoil our looks.

In olden days the lane was clean
Not like it is today,
When people who just pass along
Throw their garbage along the way.

Oh, how we now are yearning
For the times that once have been,
When people cared about hedges
Keeping us trim and green.

OUR GARDENS

We once had a garden neat and small
Surrounded by a flintstone wall,
We grew snowdrops and crocuses in the spring
Listened to songbirds on the wing.

That is all a long time ago,
We have gardened in many places,
But that little old garden of ours
Still puts a smile on our faces.

We were young and worked together,
Tending everything we grew,
And we were amazed again each time
When we grew something new.

Now we still love our garden,
Growing snowdrops like years ago,
We talk of our little old garden,
But now we mostly mow.

SNOWDROPS

One morning walking in the rain
Along a Devon country lane
I spotted something small and white
In the early morning light.

It was a humble snowdrop
Swaying gently in the breeze,
Its little white bell on a fragile stem
Adding to the colour of the frieze.

A frieze of dark green verges,
Of hedges and the odd tree,
Of empty brown fields across the hedge
As far as the eye could see.

I stopped and looked at the snowdrop,
I thought I could hear its bell ring,
I felt so very lucky
To see this harbinger of spring.

NATURE

I was driving through a forest
One dark cold autumn night
The clouds obstructed the moon on and off,
Producing an eerie light.

I stopped to listen to the quiet
Of this lovely autumn night,
When all at once I heard a noise
That really gave me a fright.

It was an awful roaring sound
Like I had never heard before
Accompanied by crackling wood
Roar echoing after roar.

I looked along the road to see
What it could possibly be
But even my full headlights
Could not enlighten me.

Then I remembered the story I had heard
In the local, told by mine host,
Who would spin an unbelievable yarn
Of a headless roaring ghost.

I closed my window, intending to go
When I spotted the cause of the roar
Two magnificent stags in the road
Ready to go to war.

They were tearing into each other,
Antlers locking tight,
Each attacking the other
Trying to win the fight.

I had never seen such a wonderful sight
In all my earlier life
Two animals fighting to the death,
In order to win a wife.

They finally finished the battle,
With one of them running away,
The other one issuing a victory roar;
I remember it to this day.

How wonderful it was to see
Such a magnificent natural sight
I started up the engine
And forgot the ghostly fright.

THE OLD OAK TREE

Deeply anchored in the red soil
Of the Devon countryside
Stood an oak tree tall and solid
With its branches spreading wide.
Has it been there long?
Who had made it strong?
Who had made it grow so tall?
Why did it grow at all?

When first I saw it it stunned me
It was so beautiful,
Its mighty crown widely spread out
Was such a sight to see
I wondered who had planted it,
How long had it been part of the scene?
What storms had it weathered in its life?
And what events had it seen?

I asked some of the locals,
How long it had been there
But not one of them could tell me,
Which really was quite rare
As a rule there is mostly
A story or two to be told,
When there is an oak as large as this,
An oak so very old.

I never found out how old it was,
Perhaps I shall one day,
But that will be more difficult now

That the oak has been taken away.
It was felled in the cause of progress,
Man had to build a road
So he could travel faster
Hastening the travel mode.

All I can say, it's a pity
For the old oak to have been cut down,
Each time I look at the place where it stood
I still see its mighty crown.

A SILVER POCKET WATCH

My granddad bought a pocket watch around 1899,
This is the story of this watch, a watch that is now mine.
My granddad died many years ago, in nineteen thirty three
He left instructions that the watch should finally come to me.

I was only six when Granddad died,
But I remember it quite clear
Whenever we visited Granddad
He held it to my ear
To hear the clock:
Tick tock, tick tock, tick tock.

Many years have passed since then,
But I still have Granddad's clock,
My daughter used to listen to its beat,
Tick tock, tick tock, tick tock.

Dad gave it to me when I left home
To serve my country in war,
But when I was taken prisoner
I thought I would see it no more.

When I was searched they never found
Dear old Granddad's watch,
I had hidden it in a dressing
That was quite close to my crotch.

The watch was my constant companion,
It always kept good time,
But one day it gave up the ghost
Without any reason or rhyme.

I took it to a watchmaker
Who looked at it and said:
"This watch is beyond repair my friend,
The main spring now is dead".

I thanked him and took the watch home
To try to seek second advice,
But I forgot it for a while
Looking at it once or twice.

A year or two later I met a man
To whom I related my tale.
Nonsense, he said, I shall mend it for you
And render it hearty and hale.

Ever since then Granddad's watch
Has been ticking away,
Keeping good time once again
For me, day after day.

It really is a lovely clock
As my grandchildren can tell
Like me they listened to its tick tock,
And my great-grandsons as well.

Now if Granddad up there in heaven
Can see his lovely old clock
He'll smile to himself saying:
"I hope they will always be listening
To my old watch going 'tick tock'.

TROY

When dawn with rosy fingers lit up the eastern sky
A battle-weary warrior on the lofty walls of Troy
Surveyed the plain that lay below, the scene of many a fight
Littered with bodies of friend and foe, united in their plight.

He gazed up to the heavens, to the immortals in the sky
To ask the noblest of them all to tell him the reason why
Men had to fight each other, spill their life's blood in the sand,
Killing foe and brother, and when will it ever end?

Zeus, sitting on his lofty throne, just shook his wise old head
Lightning flashed and thunder rolled, and this is what he said:
"Brave warrior listen to my words, for all that they are worth
There will always be killing and wars as long as man lives on earth.

While there is the constant need
Of your leaders for booty and greed
They will tell you to be loyal and brave,
While they are digging your grave.

The sky lit up, and once again the warrior had to fight,
Weapons clashed, the wounded screamed, the plain was set alight.
The warrior fell and lay on his back, his eyes stared at the sky,
They seemed to ask one last question: Why?

THE BATTLE OF HALBE, APRIL 1945; WHY?

The war was almost over,
April nineteen forty-five
All I could think of, like everyone else
Was how to stay alive.

One day I was sent out on a recce,
A young man all alone
To discover if there was a way
We could break out and make for home.

I wasn't really worried,
Having done this sort of job before,
But the war was nearly over,
I didn't want to do it any more.

We had been in this cauldron
Now for a day or two,
Soviet forces all around us
Would we ever be able to break through?

I crossed a path in the forest
And on the other side
At the foot of a gnarled old tree
I discovered a gruesome sight.

Lying there, stretched out on his back
Was a young man just like me
He was wearing a Russian uniform,

He was dead, it was plain to see.
His eyes of blue were staring
Wide open at the sky
I could almost hear the young soldier's voice
Asking the question: why?

For centuries through man's history
Men always had to fight,
I'm sure that it will never stop
Even though it isn't right.

I consider myself lucky
To have survived the war,
That I wasn't lying like my fellow man
Not to go home any more.

Why can't we stop all this fighting?
Why do we have to wage war?
Why can't we be kind to each other?
Life would be worth so much more.

THE A30 BYPASS, 1994

They planned to construct a bypass
To ease the traffic flow
From Exeter to Honiton,
Fifteen miles and two years to go.

First they cut down trees and hedges,
Dug a trench through the fields by hand,
Raised mounts to accommodate bridges
Thoroughly scarring the land.

Then they burnt all the trees and hedges
Right along the fifteen miles,
Not caring for the environment
Heaping the cuttings in piles.

Alas the destruction was senseless,
Parliament postponed the scheme,
But they couldn't bring back trees and hedges
It was just like a terrible dream.

Now hear this, it is the latest,
They are going private now
It's build now, get paid later,
Another public row?

Meanwhile there is still no improvement,
Traffic jams happen again,
Next summer once more no movement,
All seems to have been in vain.

But that is not the end of the story,
The bypass has now been built
The dreams of no more hold-ups
Have finally been fulfilled.

It does not take long to reach Exeter now,
But that's where the trouble starts,
Because there are always times of the day
When the traffic stands still in some parts.

HOW TO LIVE FRUGALLY

Today I read with some dismay
How much food we throw away,
That what it says in the press.
Here is another fine mess.

The honorary member of the House
No doubt living in luxury
Is telling his constituents
To live their lives more frugally.

He talks of veggies in the fridge
Of cheese wrapped up to keep fresh,
He thinks he knows frugality
While getting his pound of flesh.

I'm surprised he has not thought
Of better ways to save food,
Let me suggest rationing
Perhaps it would do us all good.

Just think what it would do to us,
Not only would we save money,
We would become a nation of "skinnies"
Wouldn't that be funny?

THE CORRUPT POLITICIAN

Now here is a little story
About a "true blue" Tory
Who broke all the rules,
Thinking people are fools
In his quest for riches and glory.

One day he was out of luck,
All his plans became unstuck,
He bragged to the press,
Got himself in a mess,
In fact he scored a duck.

Up to now life had been fine,
But now he had to resign
From his job in the Tory party,
But he remained hale and hearty,
Promising to toe the line.

However it's not only the Tories
That appear to break many rules,
Politicians of other parties
Also take voters for fools.

HEY DIDDLE DIDDLE

(An alternative version)

Hey Diddle Diddle, MPs on the fiddle
Politicians don't care at all,
The people in charge are the men in grey suits
Scheming out of Whitehall.

These people however
Like me and you
Take their orders silently
From the moguls of the EU.

This country once had a democracy,
But alas it has it no more,
We are just told to do this and do that
As it never has been before.

Immigrants now do all the work,
To hire them is so very cheap,
While many of us who can't find a job,
Are just thrown on the rubbish heap.

Just like in the old dictatorships
We now are just pawns of the state,
Living our lives with daily thoughts
Of what will be our fate.

The latest idea I read of today
Is the thought of a bedroom tax,
If your home is considered too big for you
Take lodgers, or pay tax.
If you are old and the doctor you see
He will give you a simple test
To establish the state of your senility,
I'll let you guess the rest.

Social workers will say you are not fit
To be left by yourself to roam,
They will make an order to send you off
To some old people's home.

There you no longer can be yourself,
You'll be told just what to do,
When to get up and when to sit still,
And when your bedtime is due.

So there you are being cared for
By people you don't understand,
For they have not mastered the language
Of this once-pleasant democratic land.

I think I have made myself clear,
Having said what is written above,
Let's get rid of this dictatorship,
Let's live our lives in love.

GREEN FIELDS NO MORE

These pleasant green and fertile lands
Are slowly being turned to brown,
Each village has some development
That will soon turn it into a town.

Why do we spoil this pleasant land?
Why do we feel the need?
Is it because folks are homeless?
Or is it some people's greed?

I don't know what possesses them
That they want to spoil village life,
Where people know each other,
Live peacefully without much strife.

What could be more pleasant than a walk
Between hedges of luscious green,
Meet other people, stop for a talk,
And admire the wonderful scene?

Some people have lived here all their lives
Others moved here to enjoy
The peaceful village life
Which others now wish to destroy.

I say, don't let them do it,
No dwellings on fertile fields,
One day we may all be in need of the land
And the food that it can yield.

Let us yield food not houses,
Let us enjoy nourishing food,
Let us enjoy what was handed to us,
A village life that is good.

HORSESHOE BLUES

When I was having chemo, everything I ate
Tasted just like metal, oh, how I did hate
That awful nasty taste,
Lots of my food went to waste.

At last I have discovered
Why everything tasted like that
It must have been a horse's meat
I'm sure that's what I had.

Whoever slaughtered the poor thing
Forgot to pull off the shoes,
That's why my food tasted like metal,
And I wrote the "Horseshoe Blues".

THE BATTLE OF
WOUNDED KNEE

Dear oh dear, oh dearie me,
Janet Seal has hurt her knee
While out working on her plot,
And she says "It hurts a lot".

So off she went to Ottery Town
To see her GP, Dr Brown
Who said "Now let me see,
What's the trouble with your knee?"

She looked at it and prodded it,
And said "No doubt it will swell,
And there is bound to be some pain
As you know very well.

"I can only see one remedy,
To improve your injured knee,
That is to try to refer you
To physiotherapy.

"It is difficult to obtain
A fast appointment date,
As the waiting list is very long,
I'm afraid you'll have to wait."

But Janet did not want to wait,
So she thought of another choice,
She chose alternative therapy,
Booking in with her healer, Joyce.

You ask, did her knee get better?
I really do not know,
You'll just have to wait and see
Until Joyce has had a go.

MISTY'S TALE

Mrs Jones had a horse
Named Misty, it was grey,
She used to ride along our lane,
Never missing a day.
We used to see her passing our house
Come sunshine or come rain,
But one afternoon last week
We looked for her in vain.

Today we saw Mrs Valerie Jones,
She had a sad tale to tell.
She said that for the last day or two
Misty had not been well,
It appeared she had caught a virus
Making her breathe hard and sweat
So the only remedy for Misty
Was to visit the local vet.

So off they went in their horsebox
To the vet in the next town,
He examined her in her horsebox,
As Misty was lying down.
He shook his head and hummed and hawed,
Took her temperature and said
"I think it must be a virus,
Which could really be quite bad.

"So I'm afraid she'll have to stay
With us for a day or two
Mrs Jones, I'm really sorry

For the worry it's causing you."
"Never mind" said Val to the doctor,
"Just try to save my dear horse,
I know that you will do your best,
And I shall be grateful of course."

Now Misty was at the hospital,
Suffering injections and drips,
And Val, in spite of all her work
Undertook daily hospital trips.
Gradually Misty got better,
Enjoying her sugar beet
It seemed that within a few days
Misty was back on her feet.

She came home at last and we saw her
Passing our house again,
It is so lovely to see her and Val
Riding once more down our lane.
Now Valerie was over the moon,
She had Misty back at home,
She had missed her so very much
At last they could once again roam.

The moral of the story is
That love between beast and man
Is one of the loveliest things on earth,
That's existed since time began.

SPRING

Dark winter evenings have gone,
Spring is here at last,
The cold and frosty nights
Are once again in the past.

Fields and hedges are green once again,
Spring flowers are in full bloom,
Masses of snowdrops and daffodils
Brighten up many a living room.

March winds are blowing
All the grey clouds away,
The warmth of the sun gets stronger
From now on every day.

When I got up this morning
I watched the rise of the sun,
And I said to myself: "How wonderful
That winter at last has gone".

SUMMER

Spring is almost over now
Summer will soon be here,
With its bright blue skies, its brilliant sun
It's a wonderful time of the year.

Birds are winging their way through the air,
Through the warm summer air in a rush,
We see skylarks high above,
And we hear the song of the thrush.

Children will soon be on holiday
Frolicking in the sun,
Kicking balls and riding their bikes
Having lots of fun.

Most of us think of holidays,
At home or in foreign lands
Of cruising, flying or just rambling
And of beaches of golden sand.

Every year has its seasons,
Spring, summer winter and fall,
But for most of us, whether young or old
Summer is best of all.

I look back on many summers
Now I am old and grey,
For me there is nothing better
Then a sunny summer's day.

AUTUMN

The days are getting short again,
Leaves are turning to gold,
Swallows are flying to the south
To warmer climes, we are told.

Fields look bare now the harvest is over
The ploughed land looks dark and cold,
Hedges are cut and ditches cleared
And tales of the past are told.

It won't be long now till winter's here,
The land will be covered in snow,
And people will say "We wish we could fly
To warm climes, where swallows go."

WINTER

Trees are bare now, cold winds blow,
All the leaves are on the ground,
Song birds have gone, the skies are grey,
It feels empty all around.

I looked at the stars in the shining sky,
Thinking of years now gone by
When other people in far-off days
Looked at the sky with far-off gaze.

What did they think of the winter world
Which then before their eyes unfurled?
Did they think of years to come?
Or like me of years that long had gone?

Whatever they thought, they must have wondered
Who created this wonderful sight
For what could be more beautiful
Then a starry winter's night?

WINTER JOYS

Do you remember the winters
Of many years ago,
When we were young and carefree
Frolicking in the snow?

I remember them vividly,
Skating on frozen lakes,
Sledging down snow-covered slopes,
Trying to dodge snowflakes.

Those were the days when we were young
Never feeling the cold,
When our elders were all reminding us
"Just wait till you get old!"

But now we are the old ones,
Wrapping up not to feel the cold,
One really feels the icy blast
When one is frail and old.

Oh, what it would be to be young again,
To frolic and slide again in the snow,
But we are not, and that is good
For we had our fun years ago.